Piaffer and Passage

Professeur

THOROUGHBRED

by *Jacobi* out of *Sainte-Enimie*

September 1931

B O O K   T H R E E

THE MASTERS OF HORSEMANSHIP
S E R I E S

PIAFFER & PASSAGE

◆

GENERAL DECARPENTRY

TRANSLATED BY
PATRICIA GALVIN

The Masters of Horsemanship Series, Book Three

Piaffer and Passage by General Decarpentry

© 1998 Half Halt Press, Inc.

First published in England in 1964 by J.A. Allen & Co., London, © P. Galvin 1961
Original design by Lawton Kennedy

Published in the United States of America by
Half Halt Press, Inc.
P.O. Box 67
Boonsboro, MD 21713

Printed in the United States of America

ISBN 0-939481-51-0

Library of Congress Cataloging-in-Publication Data

Decarpentry, général (Albert-Eugèhe-Edouard), 1878-1956.
    [Piaffer et passage. English]
    Piaffer & passage / general Decarpentry ; translated by Patricia
Galvin.
        p.   cm. -- (The masters of horsemanship series ; bk. 3)
    Originally published: London : J.A. Allen & Co., 1964. With new
photos.
    Includes bibliographical references.
    ISBN 0-939481-51-0
    1. Haute école (Horsemanship)   I. Title.   II. Series.
SF309.57.D4313   1998
    798.2'3--dc21
                                                98-22033
                                                CIP

Editors' Note

When given the privilege of publishing a classic work such as Piaffer and Passage, one of the first issues the publisher must consider is exactly what to do with such a work as far as handling the available material is concerned. Should it be "updated?" Revised in some way, an annotated version perhaps?

What about old photos where the originals have long since been lost and cannot be fully reconstructed? The photos herein date from the early 1930's and subsequent editions have lost a bit each time they have been reproduced, rather like a photocopy of a photocopy of a photocopy.

Our decision was to let the work stand as a facsimile edition and not to "improve" it. It is the outline of the horse and rider which are most important in the photos, rather than fine details of, say, the rider's boot against the horse's side, and to "update" with new photos seemed somehow irreverent.

We hope you agree.

Note on the Translation

Many equestrian terms are as elusive as their definitions. For the purposes of this text, new terms have been adopted for those which have no precise English translation. I would like to specify two of special importance, with their more classical French definitions:

BALANCE IN HAND (*mise en main*) means a light and supple contact with the mouth of the horse in complete submission to the hand of the rider. There must be neither resistance of the horse's weight (a passive resistance resulting from a faulty equilibrium, with too much weight on the forehand) nor of the horse's force (an active resistance of the muscles in the neck and jaw). The horse may be *balanced in hand* keeping the natural carriage of his head and neck, as long as he has this light and willing communication with the rider's hand.

THE GATHERING (*ramener*) concerns the position of the forehand. The horse must have a supple and elevated neck, flexion at the poll, and a loose and relaxed jaw. These conditions result in an approximately vertical position of the head.

When the horse is *gathered*, he is also *balanced in hand*, but he may be *balanced in hand* without being *gathered*.

P. G.

Foreword

By COLONEL DANLOUX

Ecuyer en chef à l'Ecole de Saumur

PIAFFER AND PASSAGE comes at the right time and answers a precise purpose: to facilitate the task of riders preparing for the difficult Olympic test.

Working alone as they usually do, they only achieve mediocre results in these two movements.

They lack a guide to lead them on the road of progress.

They will certainly find the best of counsel in these few pages, dictated by experience and written so temperately and clearly, in which the author, with a sincerity and modesty that do him credit, does not hesitate to criticize his own performance in order to make himself better understood.

You, my dear Decarpentry, are especially qualified to treat this difficult subject.

When you and I were *sous-écuyers* together, and most of us were doing more d'Aure than Baucher, were you not already trying to pierce the mysteries of *"gathering"*? And at Saumur twenty years later, in your brilliant and precise work with your horse *Professeur*, have I not found you forever aiming, above all, at perfect lightness?

Now, sending me the proofs of your treatise, you have been kind enough to ask me for a preface; may these lines from your old friend serve the purpose, plain though they be.

P. DANLOUX

Table of Contents

Piaffer and Passage

Introduction

Foreign critics agree in acknowledging the high quality of the work at the gallop presented by nearly all the French contestants in international dressage tests.

They are also unanimous in qualifying the piaffer and the passage of the same competitors, except for a few very brilliant exceptions, in less flattering terms.

Our piaffer is often scored as "sketchy," "indicated," "satisfactory," or "even"; its high and ample style (in a word, its stateliness) never rouses the enthusiasm of the critics who are often unstinted in praise of our changes of leg at every stride, for example.

But this is not surprising, since the courses at Saumur for *sous-lieutenants* and *lieutenants* go as far as the changes of leg at the gallop but exclude instruction in the piaffer and the passage.

Most of our competitors have taken only these two courses and consequently are less prepared to complete the training of their horses at the trot than at the gallop.*

It has seemed to me that it would be useful for them to have a program based on the precepts of our great masters in equitation. I have appended a few observations on putting these precepts into practice in the form of critical notes accompanying photographs of a certain horse and a certain rider with whose shortcomings I am only too well acquainted.†

*The complete course, which comprises teaching the whole of classical equitation, has only recently been instituted, and is taken by a very small number of officers. [1932.]

†[All the photographs are of Colonel Decarpentry and his horse *Professeur*, taken at the Ecole de Cavalerie in Saumur by Blanchaud.]

The Preferable Order in which to Begin these Two Movements

The rule laid down by the old school, and by that of Baucher, was to undertake first the piaffer, and then, with forward impulsion, the passage.

On the other hand, Fillis and Saint-Phalle first undertook the passage, which they then slowed down to the piaffer.

Beyond question, these movements can be brought to perfection by either method when they are taught to the horse by a master.

For horsemen of less skill, however, and in view of the present dressage tests of the Fédération Equestre Internationale, the practice of the old school is to be preferred for the following reasons:

1. The style of the passage as developed from the piaffer is in general more academic and conforms more closely to the definition of the Fédération Equestre Internationale in the lifting of the forearms, the bending of the knees, the vertical position of the cannons, and the raising of the fore and hindlegs in relation to each other, whereas the passage developed from the trot is more extended than elevated and is less classic in style.

2. Certain irregularities of diagonal gaits, often nearly imperceptible at the trot, are still difficult to discern in the passage even though they *always* become worse in that movement and only appear clearly in the piaffer.

When the piaffer is developed from the passage, and consequently is a result of long-continued work during which these irregularities have become established by habit, it is very difficult to correct them—if it is not already too late to succeed in doing so.

By beginning, on the contrary, with the piaffer, it is easier to notice the irregularities in the diagonals and to correct them before they become permanent.

I propose to set forth the preparation and gradual perfecting of the piaffer, and then the development of the passage from the piaffer.

The program that I present seems to me, among ways of achieving the piaffer, the logical extension and complement of the training methods used by the majority of our military riders, most of whom I have been in a position to observe for many years.

When to Begin the Training for the Piaffer

The training for the piaffer should be commenced when the horse is completely schooled at the walk and trot.

It is essential that without change of his *balance in hand* the horse can execute the following:

1. Changes in pace at the trot and *especially: the depart from a standstill to a trot, and the direct halt from a trot.*

2. Work on both hands; in particular, the small volte at the trot with the haunches in.

To help make matters clear I am adopting the following definitions:

BALANCE IN HAND—Absolute submission of the jaw *in the gathering,* characterized by "its yielding softly . . . to the first request of the hand" (General L'Hotte).

THE GATHERING—A vertical, or nearly vertical, position of the head, *the poll always being the highest point of the head and neck.*

HALF HALT—A firm upward movement on *tightened* reins, with fingers *well closed,* quickly followed by progressive opening of the fingers and giving with the hand.

This action is analogous to that of heaving up a heavy stone from the foot of a staircase and putting it gently down on one of the steps *without damaging* its surface and without noise.

[8]

How to Prepare for the Piaffer

Execute alternately, at first with fairly long intervals, the following two exercises:

1. From a standstill, depart at the trot, follow with a halt.

2. Halt from a trot, follow with a depart at the trot.

In the first of these exercises the number of steps be-

[9]

tween the depart and the halt is to be reduced progressively.

The measure of this reduction is governed always by the *balance in hand*; the moment this changes, the horse is not yet supple enough to pass as quickly as is wanted from motion to a standstill and vice versa.

The reduction should therefore be made gradually.

In the second exercise the length of time in the halt should also be shortened progressively.

The conservation of the *balance in hand* will again indicate the measure of the reduction of time between the halt and the depart.

The trot should be rather slow, but definite and well marked.

The halt and depart should be rigorously straight.

When the horse can execute without loss of *balance in hand* each of these two exercises—a few steps at the trot and a halt of a few seconds, repeated five or six times in succession—the series should be finished with a longer trot followed by a prolonged halt, confirming the *balance in hand* by closing the fingers; and concluded with a long rest on the spot with the reins dropped on the horse's neck.

During these exercises it is important to observe scrupulously the rule, "Hands without legs, legs without hands," which means:

Never increase the pressure of the hands and legs *at the same time*.

If the *hand* acts or increases its action, the *leg* should either maintain the intensity of its action or decrease it, as the case requires; but the leg *should never increase its action* while the hand is acting or increasing its action.

If the leg is active or increasing its action, the hand should remain passive or give, as the case requires.

The contact of heel with flank and of hand with mouth should be close enough for the movements of hand and leg to follow one another smoothly, without interruption.

At the stage of training which the horse should now have reached, increases of the aids necessary to obtain the results wanted are very slight, and *easing* of the passive aid generally serves no useful purpose; it is sufficient not to increase it in direct and simultaneous opposition to the active aid.

If, however, the horse is going to sleep on his feet, push him forward with the leg while giving freely with the hand.

If the horse becomes heavy on the hand, make a half halt, easing the leg pressure.

Then begin again: leg active, hand fixed; hand active, leg fixed.

Avoid errors in position, especially, when the hand is active, that of leaning back too far with shoulders and chest, which would put an extra weight on the horse's haunches.

Keep the body vertical, with spurs, hips, and shoulders in line; put more weight on the stirrups and less in the seat when the horse's hindquarters diminish in their action.

Avoid errors of the hand: passing too abruptly from activity to passivity, or vice versa. The extent of these movements should be strictly limited to what is necessary and should become imperceptible when the horse is ready to begin the piaffer.

Avoid similar errors of the leg.

How to Begin the Piaffer

Alternate, as before, the action of the hand and of the leg, going from one to the other as soon as the first has begun to take effect and *before the effect is completed.*

As soon as the horse starts to move under the action of the leg, which relaxes immediately, with the *hand* restrain his advance *without stopping the movement.*

As soon as the horse tends to become immobile under the action of the hand, give instantly, and use the *leg* to prevent a *complete cessation of the movement*—and so on.

After a few alternating movements, let the horse go forward freely by using the leg, and then, after a good trot, bring him to a definite halt with the hand and give him a long rest on the spot.

After a certain number of sessions the horse will begin to keep the cadence of the trot while scarcely advancing at each step.

Let him continue by himself for a few seconds, but take care to avoid letting him stop by himself; the exercise should always be concluded *at the command of the rider,* whether by halting or by going forward in a trot.

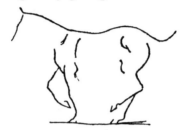

The general posture of the horse is cramped during these first exercises. The vertebral column is not sufficiently shortened, as it should be by flexion throughout. The ensemble of neck and trunk extends too far to the front and the rear of the base of support of the legs, which converge excessively beneath the body.

The upper part of the body is contracted, and the loins are arched.

The rider feels lifted above the horse. His knees are pushed up by the expansion of the ribs, which at the same time causes the flanks to draw in and seemingly shrink from contact with the rider's calves.

The contraction of the croup muscles provokes a rather violent twitching of the tail.

The hindlegs are lifted too far forward, with insufficient flexion at the stifle and the hock.

[14]

The forelegs strike the ground too far back.

In each diagonal on the ground the horse's feet are too close together, making the base of support too short for him to trust himself on it for long, with the result that the legs are not raised enough and the alternating of the diagonals is often hurried.

The neck is generally too low and the angle at the poll too wide. The mouth loses its suppleness, or, more often, nervously exaggerates its mobility.

Developing the Piaffer

When calm prevails in the trot *almost* on the spot, when the regularity of the beat is asserted, and when the twitching of the tail is subsiding, the rider should begin to modify the general posture of the horse by raising his head and neck in the *gathered* position.

RAISING THE HEAD AND NECK.—This should be undertaken first, and continued gradually, until the end of

NOTE: *See the photograph*—"DEVELOPMENT OF THE PIAFFER" *page 33.*

the nose is almost on a level with the point of the haunches, the *balance in hand* and the *gathering* remaining unchanged.

As long as this result is obtained only under *persistent* action of the hand, and ceases with it, it must be deemed inadequate.

The horse should hold this position *of his own accord*, and not seek to modify it before he is asked to do so.

The raising of the head and neck lessens by degrees the amount of advance at each step, often to the point that the horse will continue the movement on the spot.

If this result is not yet completely attained, the rider should not feel disturbed. The work at raising the forelegs will achieve the reduction of the forward movement.

Usually, however, the horse tends to move slightly backward rather than to continue on the spot.

Unless the backward movement is unquestionably a sign of unwillingness bordering on defense, the horse should not be corrected with the spur; instead, he should be brought forward with a measured pressure of the leg, without interruption of the rhythm. This should be repeated each time he tries to find his balance by drawing back.

THE GATHERING.—The vertical position of the head can only be maintained, when the neck is raised, by increased flexion at the poll.

When the position is obtained with perfect *balance in hand*, that is, through *voluntary* obedience, it reacts on the entire vertebral column and increases its supple flexion throughout.

The distance between nose and tail is thus decreased and the body extends less to the front and the rear of the legs, which, moreover, are brought closer together by their *upper* extremities. The horse, therefore, while remaining collected, has his legs less drawn beneath him.

The back relaxes and lowers, with the result that the haunches and the point of the buttocks are also lowered, and consequently the stifle joint and hock.

The tail becomes still and rounded.

When the forelegs touch the ground they are almost in line vertically with the top of the withers; and similarly, the hindlegs with the point of the haunches.

The horse's balance on the diagonals is steadier, since the base of support they give to the body is more in proportion to its length.

The horse gains confidence in the exercise and his steps become well spaced.

Raising the Forelegs

When the horse is calm and confident in this position, with no alteration of his *balance in hand* or of the cadence, and without trying to lower his neck or change the *gathering*, the rider can begin to raise the forelegs, gradually bringing the forearms to the level of the point of the elbow.

This is achieved by putting weight on the foreleg that is on the ground, prolonging the time on this diagonal.

To keep his balance, the horse will lift the other foreleg and prolong the period of its suspension.

By putting pressure on the horse's neck with the right

NOTE: *See the photograph*—"DEVELOPMENT OF THE PIAFFER" *page 33.*

[21]

rein, for example, weight can be shifted to the left shoulder from the right.

This result follows only when the horse obeys the rein without evasion and commits himself confidently to his action.

In the beginning, this is not usually the case: instinctively the horse will try to escape the pressure by contracting in various ways, the most frequent of which are the following:

A. He more or less refuses to bend his neck in the direction demanded. The effect of the rein, instead of controlling the forehand as required, is transmitted down the spinal column to the left hindleg and more or less paralyzes it.

The cadance is lost, first of all in the hindquarters.

B. He flexes his neck almost to the degree demanded, but does it by turning his head to the right.

The transfer of weight to the left sought by the rider is slight or not effected, since the right shoulder has not been sufficiently lightened.

The hindquarters, affected by the rein as before, again lose the rhythm, and the movement of the horse becomes more or less disturbed.

C. He flexes his neck almost to the degree demanded, but does so by drawing his withers to the left. The left shoulder is then too far to the side for the left foreleg to stay in place, and that leg will move abruptly back under the shoulder.

The cadence is lost, first in the forehand.

[22]

It is hardly possible to escape all these instinctive reactions, but one should avoid provoking them. This can be done, up to a point, by tact in the demands made by the hand, but above all by the CORRECT TIMING of these demands.

Pressure on the right rein before the left foreleg touches the ground will move the placing of that foot to the left. And the result is the same if the pressure is continued until the leg is raised.

Therefore, the interval of time within which the effect of the rein can produce the desired result in an orderly way is very limited.

Moreover, the rider must possess perfectly that *feeling for the lifting and lowering* of the horse's feet which the *écuyer* Aubert considered to be the basis of tact.

He should also have developed his skill in balancing the horse between the different demands of the same rein; and no exercise is better for this than alternating a shoulder-in with a two-track, as described so precisely by Commandant de Salins in his two works known to all.*

While practicing, it is therefore necessary:

1. Never to try to bend the horse when he is not perfectly *balanced in hand*.

2. To be content for a long period with tightening the fingers on the right rein, the hand being well over the withers, as the left foreleg comes to the ground.

3. To rectify little by little, and by tentative trials, the amount of pressure to give the right rein so that it will

*J. de Salins, *Méthode de dressage rapide du cheval de selle et d'obstacles*, Rennes: Oberthur, 1925, and *Secret de l'art équestre (Epaule en dedans)*, Rennes: Oberthur, 1931.

[23]

transport to the left shoulder ONLY the excess weight one wants it to support, without impairing the action of the hindquarters.

4. To increase little by little the intensity and duration of the tightening of the fingers, watching the effect obtained so as to reduce their pressure at the first sign of confusion.

It is of course very important that the results obtained are exactly equal for both shoulders. Nevertheless, in the beginning it is usually necessary to work on only one of them while the horse takes several steps. Practice may even be restricted to one shoulder for quite a while.

As soon, however, as the rider obtains the slightest hint of lightness on one side, he should quickly seek the same result on the other. One shoulder may require more time than the other, since horses, like human beings, are never exactly symmetrical by nature.

Next, the rider should combine the two movements until the steps of the forelegs are exactly equal and made at a somewhat slower pace than at the start of the exercise.

Then he should begin working again on each shoulder separately.

Throughout these exercises the action of the hand should cease as soon as the horse loses impulsion.

The leg should then be used, without abruptness but firmly if need be, until the diagonals definitely regain their rhythm.

The leg is then to be relaxed and the action of the hand resumed.

Developing the Fullness of Movement

The knees may flex past the right angle, leaving the cannons behind the vertical as the forearms are raised to the horizontal.

The piaffer then loses its correctness and grace.

The cause of this faulty action is that *the forehand is not sufficiently relieved of weight*. Bringing the cannon forward would destroy the forward equilibrium, and the horse is instinctively warned of this danger.

If, in this faulty position, the horse is asked to raise his leg, he can only respond by throwing his foot toward the elbow without bringing it forward, and by exaggerated flexion of his knee.

This fault is often difficult to correct; yet it is relatively easy to avoid by not asking for an elevation of the forelegs until the forehand is sufficiently lightened to let the fore-feet *strike the ground* on a vertical with the top of the withers.

When this condition has not been fulfilled and the fore-legs have begun the cramped action, no further attempt should be made to raise them. One should recommence the exercise at the point where the awkward overflexion began.

Usually the lack of lightness in the forehand is not caused by an insufficiently raised neck, but rather by a lack in the *gathering*.

It may well be that this insufficience in the *gathering* escaped the notice of the rider well in advance of his attempt at the piaffer, and was already evident in the work at the trot, at the walk, and even at the halt.

One should therefore go back in the program of training as far as need be to remedy the error at the point where it began to appear, and to obtain a stability in the *gathering* in all the work that follows, up to the point where the exercise of raising the forelegs in the piaffer may be recommenced.

It should also be noted that the drawing back of the cannons often coincides with a tendency to back up.

This should be corrected by requiring a slight but well-marked advance at each step.

Development
of the Piaffer

*Rectifying the General Position
by Raising the Forehand*

I

USING THE HAND. —When asked to raise his head and neck, the horse resists (note the slant of the bit).

The horse is high in the croup (see profile of point of croup above joint of haunch). The point of the buttocks, the stifle, the hock, and the knee are hardly bent. The horse is *tilted forward* on his left foreleg, which is placed too far back, whereas his right foreleg is barely off the ground.

The rider is lifted up by the contraction of the back (a horizontal from the tip of the ears goes through the rider's pocket). His knees are also lifted and his legs are spread and pushed forward by the swelling of the chest (note the distance from the rider's knee to the edge of the saddle, and from his foot to the girth).

II

UsING THE HAND.—The horse yields to the hand (see the slant of the bit). His back flexes (see the lowered position of the rider: the horizontal from the tip of the ears passes above the rider's shoulder). The horse's chest deflates (see the distance from rider's knee to edge of saddle, and from his foot to the girth). The haunches are lowered (the point of the croup has disappeared; the flexion of the hindquarter joints is emphasized, as is the elevation of the suspended hindleg).

The forehand is tipped forward less (see the distance of the vertical from end of nose to tip of forefoot on ground). The forefoot in suspension leaves the ground with greater freedom. The flexion of the knee is increased.

The rider is sitting into the horse, and his legs are in the proper position.

Developing
the Action of the Forelegs

III

USING THE HAND (up and down and from right to left, to lighten the right shoulder).

There is resistance in the back, and the chest swells. The forehand gives a little, the neck swings to the right and draws back. The bent position of the foreleg on the ground shows that it is still too far back to permit a durable balance. The right foreleg is lightened and lifted, and the knee is almost on a vertical line with the ears. Because

[39]

the spine is contracted, the movement of the left hindleg is affected by the rein and reduced in action.

The rider is stiff, his torso tips back, and his legs go forward.

IV

Yielding of the hand and use of the leg to activate the hindlegs of the horse.

The back yields and the rider sits into the saddle. The croup is lowered and the joints of the hindlegs flex. The foreleg on the ground is almost vertical and has advanced closer to its proper position. The right foreleg is visibly lifted (the action as shown, however, is exaggerated because the photograph was not taken in full profile).

[41]

V

FIXITY of the hand and leg to let the horse find his own equilibrium.

Here, the horse is approaching his proper balance, as the improvement in his general position testifies, but he has not quite found it, as can be seen by his opened jaw.

He is still too high in the croup. The hindleg on the ground is well placed but insufficiently flexed, neither is the hindleg off the ground sufficiently flexed, especially at the hock, with the result that the fetlock joint is not far enough under the mass above it; nor is the foot sufficiently raised.

The foreleg on the ground is well placed (the vertical from the toe reaches the upper third of the neck).

The foreleg off the ground is correct.

The torso of the rider is too far back, which adds weight to the hindleg off the ground.

The Passage

To pass from the piaffer to the passage, obtained through the program which has just been described, one must "drop the barrier" of opposition by the rider's hand to the push of the horse's hindlegs in order to transform into a forward movement a portion of their energy spent solely in the up and down movement of the piaffer.

In general, the yielding of the hand will cause at first a marked hesitation in the horse, which must be overcome with the leg, used frankly but with moderation and without abruptness.

The horse, responding to this signal, loses his forward balance and passes into an ordinary trot after two or three somewhat rhythmical steps.

For the first few days it is desirable to let him trot freely some tens of meters without opposition of the hand, then bring him to a halt and reward him.

Then, one should continue as before, but seeking to *balance* him *in hand* as soon as the forward movement is established, and follow with a halt.

When the horse can halt easily keeping his *balance in hand*, he is to be brought to a halt as soon as the several steps of CADENCED trot following the piaffer lapse into an ordinary trot.

Finally, one passes from the piaffer into the cadenced trot, halts as soon as the cadence is lost, recommences the piaffer, passes again into the cadenced trot, and so on, until the cadenced trot is easily maintained with the horse *balanced in hand* and making no precipitate steps but advancing slowly and without hesitation.

[47]

One must be especially careful in the beginning not to start out from the horse's *"maximum"* piaffer, but on the contrary, from a less elevated piaffer that is well defined and above all perfectly calm.

Going from the piaffer to the cadenced trot demands, at least at first, an extra effort of the hindlegs.

If the elevation of the piaffer has already demanded their maximum effort, the horse will *"fall"* into a trot with no cadence instead of *"throwing"* himself into an energetic cadenced trot.

Little by little the horse acquires skill in this exercise and, in large measure, substitutes for the extra effort of the hindlegs a new balance of his body which transforms into forward movement a part of the vertical movement of the piaffer.

One can now start from a more elevated piaffer, but always with care not to allow the cadence to abate as the forward movement develops.

One must not start from a more elevated piaffer unless the cadence of the preceding one was fully maintained in the forward movement.

The cadenced trot is thus transformed little by little into the passage.

Going from Piaffer
to Passage

I

An even piaffer, but of a less elevated development than that of which the horse is capable. It is a good basis for acquiring, from the beginning, an energetic passage.

II

Too much use of the leg. The horse loses his forward balance and throws himself on the hand. In spite of this fault, the "*form*" of the passage is satisfactory.

The photograph, taken at an angle, exaggerates the gesture of the hindlegs and diminishes that of the forelegs.

The rider has allowed himself to become inert; his torso is too far back.

[53]

III

Use of the hand to restore the equilibrium (by alternating the actions of both reins).

The visible resistance of the horse's mouth corresponds to the faulty engagement of the hindleg on the ground. The legs in suspension are correct.

The rider's heels are in the air. The position of his torso is better than in the preceding photograph.

IV

The resistance to the hand has diminished, the hindleg on the ground has come forward, but the croup is too high and the loins are sunken. The foreleg on the ground is placed too far forward.

The rider's heels are even higher in the air; his torso, which is behind the movement, is thrown back and contributes to the depression of the loins.

V

The resistance has diminished even more; it has not
ceased, however, as is shown by the slant of the bit and the
opened jaw.

The general posture is better. The *gathering* and the
flexion of the loins are almost correct. The hindleg on the
ground is still not sufficiently advanced under the mass
above it and is insufficiently flexed. On the other hand, the
suspended hindleg is flexed and lifted too much, doubtless

[59]

from the request of a spur too far back and too high. The foreleg on the ground is well placed, but the foreleg off the ground is not raised enough and is not flexed enough at the knee.

The rider is very badly placed, sitting too far back with his torso behind the movement and his knees and heels up.

The Passage
Obtained from a Trot

The passage developed from the trot often has a more extended style than that developed from the piaffer, even with a horse that has been schooled first in the piaffer; but it is then easier to modify the style and bring it closer to the classic manner.

I

The horse is in his natural trot, without being collected. Through a natural defect his hindlegs always have a higher action than his forelegs when the rider does not intervene to modify this obvious imperfection of gait.

II

The *balance in hand* modifies this difference in elevation, but, being too low, is insufficient to reverse it.

III

The inversion is obtained by lowering the hindlegs and
not, as it would seem, by raising the forelegs.

IV

The foreleg is raised but the hindleg on the ground is not sufficiently engaged, with the result that the *balance in hand* and the *gathering* are lost.

V

The passage is nearing, yet not attaining, the classic style. The general position of the horse is correct but the fore-leg is not raised sufficiently, a fault further stressed by the photograph, which was not taken in full profile. The rider, however, benefits by the camera angle, which gives the impression that his position is relatively correct.

Bibliographical Note

Aside from J. de Salins, whom the author cites on page 23, writers on equitation named in preface and text of *Piaffer and Passage*, in the order of their mention, and their principal works, are:

Count d'Aure (1799-1863)
> *Traité d'équitation*, 1834; revised, 1844, 1870
> *Cours d'équitation*, 1850; rev. 1852, 1853

François Baucher (1796-1873)
> *Dictionnaire raisonné d'équitation*, 1833, rev. 1851
> *Dialogues sur l'équitation*, 1834
> *Méthode d'équitation, basée sur de nouveaux principes*, 1842, rev. 1859

James Fillis (1834-1913)
> *Principes de dressage et d'équitation*, 1890, rev. 1892
> *Journal de dressage*, 1903

Captain J.-F.-M.-J. de Saint-Phalle (1867-1908)
> *Dressage et emploi du cheval de selle*, 1899, rev. 1904
> *Equitation*, 1907

General A.-F. L'Hotte (1825-1904)
> *Un Officier de cavalerie—Souvenirs de Général L'Hotte*, 1905
> *Questions équestres*, 1906

P.-A. Aubert (ca. 1783-1863)
> *Traité raisonné d'équitation*, 1836

General Decarpentry

The preparation for the writing of *Piaffer and Passage* consists of a lifetime of dedication to dressage, a dedication rooted in the traditional values of the old school of equitation and directed to the search for the formula of the art of riding.

Born in 1878, Decarpentry came from a family of horsemen. His grandfather Eugène Caron was a pupil of Baucher. His great-uncle François Caron, the chief riding master of the Tsar of Russia, was proclaimed by Fillis to be his model. Edouard Caron, his uncle, owned a school of equitation and was the first to put the young Decarpentry in the saddle. It is not surprising that Decarpentry also had a vocation to dressage and chose a military career in the French cavalry.

For twenty years as a member of the Cadre Bleu and the Cadre Noir, eight of them in the capacity of *écuyer* at Saumur, Decarpentry was engaged in the study of d'Aure, Baucher, L'Hotte and the many other masters to whose wealth of equestrian writings he fell heir. In the examination of theories and the practical experience afforded by daily trial and error, Decarpentry not only produced beautifully schooled horses but developed and put into writing the framework of a logical and methodical program of dressage.

In 1947 Decarpentry became the President of the Dressage Commission of the Fédération Equestre Internationale and undertook the difficult task of setting the standard for, and adjusting the requirements of, international dressage competitions and of bringing strong national opinions into harmony. His success on the juries resulted in reconciling many differences of equestrian thought and, at the same time, in creating a universal ideal for the perfect dressage horse.

Drawing upon his vast knowledge and the wisdom of practical experience, Decarpentry presents the fruit of his labour in six works which in turn place him among the great masters whom he followed so faithfully.

The titles of his works:

Piaffer et passage, 1932

L'Ecole espagnole de Vienne, 1948

Baucher et son école, 1948

Equitation académique, 1949

*Les Maitres écuyers du manege de Saumur,
de 1814 a 1874*, 1954

L'Essentiel de la Méthode de haute école de Raabe,
1958